Too Skilled

Factorization of an Individual's Value

Jason T. Bevis

ISBN: 1540858847
ISBN-13: 9781540858849
Library of Congress Control Number: 2016920373
LCCN Imprint Name: CreateSpace Independent Publishing
Platform, North Charleston, SC

This book is dedicated to business leaders and to helping them understand key elements of success by leveraging those excellent employees who help make their companies rise to the top before those key players decide to leave their firms.

It is also dedicated to all you employees and A players who decided to leave companies because you felt you were undervalued or that your bosses never listened. May you find places that value your talents, or may you start companies of your own.

Finally, this book is dedicated to those individuals who have worked for me tirelessly over the years. Several of you live the Too Skilled Factor, and I thank you for helping me be successful as a leader.

Contents

Acknowledgments

Thank you to my beautiful family, especially Norma Bevis, my wife, and to Phil Cannariato for always encouraging me to be more successful than I am today. I would also like to acknowledge the elite group of friends I have in ROT8. Thank you all for supporting me in my professional and personal life. For those people and companies that provided me the pleasure of employment, I would like to acknowledge you all for the lessons in life that led me to write this book.

1. Abandon Ship

In the early part of a new year, a high-growth cybersecurity company acquires another, smaller company of fewer than twenty employees, and both companies celebrate a day of success. The larger cybersecurity company believes the new acquisition will help change the direction of cybersecurity as well as the organization, facilitating internal changes that are to help set a new direction for the industry. The employees of the acquired company are mostly happy, especially the technology-based employees, feeling their work over the past two years in this new security technology area has proved its value. The acquiring company communicates on the public earnings call with excitement that change is in progress. With this announcement, the company reaffirms to investors that a new cybersecurity direction is unleashed that will help sustain the company's proven leadership in the cybersecurity industry—an industry in which this company has been running strong over the past five years when growth was more than 100 percent year over year.

A few months after the acquisition, several of the acquired employees have many concerns. Within a short period after the acquisition, these acquired employees have become frustrated. They mention there are rumors on the street that customers are unhappy with the service and quality of the software from the acquired company.

It's likely that both the purchased and purchasing companies struggle to understand what has gone wrong. In short, it's the pressure to produce in unrealistic circumstances—in tandem with longer hours and some existing pent-up hostility—that has finally taken its toll. As a result, multiple employees from the acquired company give their notices and quit their jobs. It is too late; these employees have already passed the saving point. Now both the acquired and acquiring companies have to reassess their future together with fewer employees.

As a partial outsider to the event, I found after talking to each of the departing employees that the situation was all too familiar to some of my experiences: the value of an employee might not have been recognized. There was also some level of conflict with one employee in particular, and management never listened or took action to address the area of conflict.

It has been more than sixteen years since the first draft of the *Too Skilled Factor* was designed and written, and recent events from the acquisition have stimulated a memory of a similar situation involving multiple employees walking out the door of another company. In slightly different circumstances, there was another series of actions that ultimately influenced and inspired the idea and writing of the original transcript for *Too Skilled*.

Losing multiple employees at once should never happen, and it reflects badly on everyone in the situation. Knowing how to turn this around and ultimately prevent it is the key to strong leadership and maintaining a successful business and work environment.

In these pages are stories and values to explain the problems associated with poor leadership, inexperienced management, and the situations that cause companies to undervalue their employees and eventually lose both employees and customers. A company's success depends on its individuals and, even more important, on the few great employees that make things happen. Too Skilled is the prime factor that makes an individual of great value in association with a strong leader who can be successful in a particular situation. The *Too Skilled Factor* represents the idea that a great individual, if leveraged correctly, can significantly change the results in a positive manner and affect the outcome of various work-related scenarios.

This book was written to explain why leaders need to recognize and value exceptional employees and to further emphasize Thomas Carlyle's great-man theory. A valued employee—with the right captain—can take the ship to uncharted waters, similar to how the Chicago Bulls 1989 head coach, Phil Jackson, recognized and helped take one highly skilled individual and the team to the championship multiple times. But an undervalued employee, especially when compounded in multiples, can drive each person to abandon the mission and possibly send the company into dangerous stagnant waters.

2. The Employee-Loss Timeline

There are typically three phases of the work-life cycle before an individual quits. These phases are loyalty, communication, and loss/gain. Each of these phases is represented in figure 1 on the horizontal axis from left to right, representing the timeline of an employee's job from when he or she starts a job until that employee leaves the organization. On the vertical axis, using a curved line across these phases, is the employee's interest level in the job over time. In addition, other key employee emotions and actions, represented within the figure, will be explored further in association with the work-life cycle. These actions and emotions explain pivoting points in the cycle, such as when the employee begins presenting solutions to management.

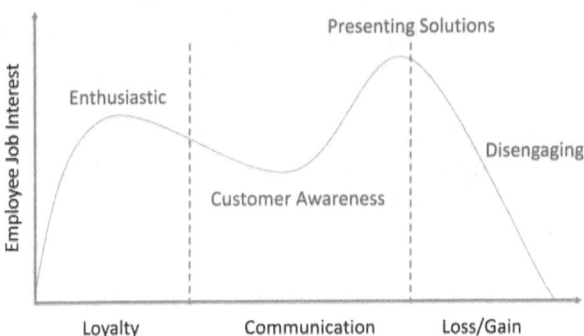

Figure 1: Employee Job-Loss Life Cycle

When an employee starts a new job, that individual is typically excited, enthusiastic, and ready to do his or her best. Most of all, the employee is loyal to the new employer and will normally spend the first three months of the new job developing a comfortable seat. The new employee is usually attentive in the new job and has great hope that the job will help lift him or her to the next career level.

After a short time, the employee has settled into the environment and has a level of understanding of both the job and the company's situation. It is at this time, after the employee has been able to assess the situation, that the employee enters the communication phase. In this phase, the leaders are typically still providing top-down communication, and the employee is attentively listening to the direction and reasoning of management and other more experienced coworkers. This time is a very critical point in the life cycle, as the employee is not only listening but has already assessed the job and wants to share his or her view.

The new employee has a keen sense of customer awareness, including the problems, which is not tainted with others' views and may offer suggestions or approaches to solve these problems. This becomes a turning point in the mind of the employee, depending on the reaction of the organization. The employee realizes either the company will foster his or her ideas and recognize the value that the employee is providing, which typically will continue to elevate that employee's success in the company, or the employer will not recognize those ideas, leading to the employee leaving.

If the manager is not aware or listening, the individual will feel there is no value in the customer-based solutions that have been presented. This is why there is a turning point when the employee presents solutions. At this turning point, the employee will either be committed to the mission and help the company succeed or start to disengage. When an employee presents a solution, the manager must communicate back to him or her. Management should either educate the employee, helping that individual grow, or empower the employee, letting him or her act on the solution. Otherwise the manager will eventually lose this person.

A good employee is normally focused on serving the customers, impressing the boss, and doing things correctly. Most new employees have an out-of-the-box mind-set, and they can often see faults in the company that are sometimes overlooked as a result of everyday business activities. This is not to say that the employee could not be completely wrong. Every situation needs to be evaluated, as inexperienced employees will sometimes need to be trained. However, if the employee is trying to contribute and see many faults in the business, that individual will want to fix those faults and make the company better.

Finally, if the employee is seeing or experiencing these problems, the employee may be pointing out an issue in the process. In this case, the value of these employees is simply providing visibility, and the business may need to look at the process, because it is likely customers are confused too. After a certain time of communicating the issues, the employee realizes no one is listening and the job is not going to change. The individual feels powerless and ultimately undervalued, and starts to remove him- or herself from the job, either emotionally or physically.

3. History of Success

Losing a great employee may have significant long-term effects on the business, such as increased cost, lost customers, or possible damage to reputation. This is a result of the company missing the Too Skilled Factor. The sport of basketball provides an excellent example of a significantly valued individual. Not every person can be compared to one of the greatest basketball players of all time—if not *the* greatest. He was a top-notch player in the game, but even top players need each team member contributions to success. Without great individuals and a program built to leverage their talents, succeeding in both sports and business is much more difficult.

To understand the essence of Too Skilled, one must examine the situation in 1984, when the Chicago Bulls had third pick at the NBA draft. The Bulls chose their star player Michael Jordan from the University of North Carolina and, just as important, rebuilt the team around him, hoping he would drive them to success. Selecting a top-draft pick and being able to win a championship season—or successfully execute a business venture—does not always work. Sometimes the formula for success requires more change, and sometimes the person is not as good as expected. With the Bulls, it wasn't until 1991 that they won their first championship, but there were many more after that year.

Too Skilled is based on the idea that one person can change the game and also drive a situation or entity to continued success. During his career, this amazing individual drove the Chicago Bulls to the playoffs every year and the team won six championships. When he played for the team, the Bulls would go to the playoffs regularly, and twice the Bulls had a "threepeat" championship series. In between the two threepeat series of championships, he retired for personal reasons, and the Bulls lost. Still to this day, since his second retirement, the Bulls have not won another championship. Eventually, when this individual left, a cascade effect occurred, and the team completely fell apart.

A situation like this is catastrophic in both sports and business. In sports, this can also happen as a result of the longevity of the athlete's career. In business, not only will an employee be lost, but customers may potentially take their business elsewhere, and other employees will exit too. This can be devastating to small businesses. In some cases, the reputation of the company is smeared, and typically a good deal of money must be spent to replace the employees to satisfy the customers. These costs may include the hiring and onboarding of a new employee, loss of productivity, and additional personnel support required as a result of the customer service issues associated with the introduction of a new hire.

Many companies are successful, but what is not apparent is that a great deal of this success is based on a few individuals who drive results and make things happen. Take a look at start-up companies, as these are typically very small teams of talented individuals. Each individual employee is critical to getting the company off the ground and plays a pivotal role in the success of the firm. One bad player in the mix can determine the difference between an Initial Public Offering (IPO) and going bankrupt.

Now look at the other end of the scale, where you have a company like Apple. The original CEO of Apple, Steve Jobs, proved time after time to be the key person who took the company to a new level every time. Unless there is another individual within Apple who can be leveraged like the him, then Apple will likely fall into the rut of a slow company that can no longer innovate or drive the market.

Even though an individual can help drive an organization's success, there are also many obstacles that must be overcome that will be discussed in the following chapters. Some of these obstacles, such as too much overhead or internal politics, are the enemies of success. Both overhead and politics make it difficult for the great individual to bring change, innovation, and success.

In some cases, even with great leaders, the structures within the organization make it difficult to navigate the process to reward the right individuals. In the case of the great basketball player, he had an excellent coach who saw a strategy to build around this player. The coach also empowered this individual to drive down the court each time, allowing him to make decisions on the fly to get the ball in the basket, ultimately winning several championships.

4. Reasons to Leave

To understand the reasons an excellent employee might leave, it is important to provide a few scenarios of actual events that have led employees to leave organizations. To help provide context for each scenario, I will explain the history of the original draft of this document.

Too Skilled was first written in January 2000. Back then, I believed I was an excellent employee who was significantly undervalued. However, this book was not written to complain about previous jobs. As I mentioned, it was written to explain why leaders need to recognize and value those key employees as well as help drive an organizational structure that promotes the value of key individuals. Otherwise, there may be bigger problems within some of these companies as a result of fostering incorrect values. This was the case in the year 2000, when within a period of two years I had been through my third company as an employee. Two of the three I had left because the organization was holding me back at some level and not listening to what I believed were the problems and solutions.

Scenario 1: Leaving the Dream Job

My professional career started before I was even out of college, at Hewlett Packard, one of the biggest computer corporations in Loveland, Colorado. While we were in college, my friends and I talked about working at this company many times. It was a dream job to work for such a titan in the technology industry. During my time at this company, I worked in the support field, and between my second and third year, a lead engineering job opened up. I applied and was told that I was at the top of thirty candidates, and within a month, my job changed to a customer-satisfaction-escalation engineer, wherein the customers' problems came directly to me multiple times a day. Unfortunately, after six months, my inexperience as a youth, lack of position in the management chain, and the fact this was a very large company stalled my innovation. In the first two years in this department, I saw that innovation flowed as a result of the management empowering the employees to solve problems. I was able to develop simulators for other employees and offered very creative solutions to help both my coworkers and customers. However, shortly after being in the new position, I found my job had become stagnant as a result of a corporate structure in which managers required employees to serve a minimal sentence in a particular position regardless of their ability. The job was no longer challenging and I was paralyzed in the company. There was no way any of my new ideas were going anywhere soon within this department.

Sure, there was still some ability to innovate for the front lines, but that wasn't a challenge nor was it going to elevate anyone's career faster than the corporate timeline would allow. There was too much politics, and there was an underlying theory in management that people needed to work a certain amount of time in one job before being promoted to the next. In either case, my managers lacked the skills and experience to leverage me correctly in the firm, and I lacked the experience and coaching to know how to engage beyond my managers. At the same time, there was a great deal of noise about one of our competitors growing substantially and taking our customer base.

Although this employer was once the company of my dreams, I was struct with disappointment. It appeared as if the company could not breakdown the boundaries associated with the internal political structure, and many solutions were overengineered, not fully usable by the customer. Instead of capturing the key customer requirements, the company was losing ground to competitors.

After realizing that I did no more except sit and wait for the next job, I decided to leave to join a start-up company in Seattle during the dot-com boom. One of my previous coworkers was on the front lines of the dot-com boom in Seattle. After he was settled, he reached out to me and asked me to come aboard. Because the situation in my current job had me paralyzed, I accepted the start-up job and moved across several states to work for this company. If only there had been a way to provide the right management coaching to employees like me, and if there had been a communication channel for customer-facing-employees' ideas to get to the leaders who could have made a difference, the outcome might have been different.

Scenario 2: Leaving for Personal Reasons

When I was living in Seattle, it was only within a six-month period that I also recruited another top worker out of the first company. Together we worked hard and helped take this start-up company to the IPO. This company had almost everything: long hours, the freedom to express ideas, great opportunities to learn, and a small paycheck that was offset with a pile of stock options. The hope was that we would be successful and those stock options would pay out. Although my direct management was fine at this company, the leadership had in its mind the idea that anyone was replaceable. This is where I first conceived the idea for *Too Skilled*. There had to be an equation for success. I did not believe that anyone and everyone was replaceable. The Chicago Bulls had already proved that although people might be replaceable, the team couldn't win another championship without another star player. Not every part is equally swapped out.

Although the leadership's stance was not my main reason for leaving, it was one of the main considerations in the decision-making process. Eventually I left that company, telling management I left for personal reasons, and moved to New York City. I could have just as easily stayed in Seattle, but sometimes leveraging personal life gives the individual an excuse to exit an unwanted situation. It turned out that shortly after the IPO, the company went bankrupt. That same leadership made some bad decisions, the company lacked solid direction, and as a result, the company could not withstand the downturn of the market. Although I left early, everyone in the company learned a great deal from this experience, including me.

Scenario 3: Recognizing Bad Leadership

The next job was in New York City on Wall Street, working as a computer network and security engineer. Unfortunately, this next company was a mess internally. The experience was very frustrating. In fact, this was the most frustrating job and situation ever in my life. The employees were frustrated, the customers were frustrated, and even many of the managers were frustrated. The technology work was fun, but there was a lack of structure and regard for the individual employees. Several individuals worked overnight hours continually, and the company sales staff was constantly overpromising to the customer on the technical designs and work effort. There was a complete disregard for customer satisfaction, and management had no ability to implement changes requested by the employees.

This company especially lacked leadership direction and value. It ignored the fact that 80 percent of the business was dependent on about 10 percent of the employees. It was essentially one large company that had bought up seven or eight smaller companies and was trying to make them work together.

At one point the executives sent one of the New York managers up to the Connecticut office to fire the majority of the staff. This event spread significant fear through many of the existing employees. Although I really enjoyed the team of people at this job and the work that we performed, something was dramatically wrong. Because of my coworkers, this place could have been an excellent company, but in my experience, every time a firm performs large scale blanket terminations without understanding the value of individual employees, it has been a sign of the deterioration of that company. The only exception I've seen, and it is typically not a large scale layoff, is prior to a firm being acquired.

This company was no different and not in any place to be acquired. There is always a challenge with blanket terminations that must include offsetting the key employees who get the job done. Unfortunately, without that offset, these drastic changes essentially made every employee wonder who was going to be fired next. If a company was willing to chop some of the smartest people in one office, what would stop them from doing the same in the New York City office? Shortly after this event, several others and I applied at one of the Big Four accounting firms in the consulting division. It turned out there were six other people from my current company applying for similar jobs, including one of the current upper-level bosses. Every one of us, four employees and two managers, left the firm within a couple of weeks and went to the new job to work as a team.

Eventually, like the company in Seattle, this company in New York went bankrupt too. This company, for whatever reason, did not recognize the value of its staff and ignored the fundamental factors of *Too Skilled*. This company actually lost almost the entire delivery team during this transition. Even if some of these individuals were not the best employees in the bunch, there was likely at least one superstar who left. To this date I'm not sure of the management team's motivations, but for an employee, when the signs pile up this high, it is a clear sign to move on.

Scenario 4: The CFO-Run Company

At this new company, my background was received very well. Management empowered the employees to succeed at their own will. In a Big X consulting firm, it is essentially feast or famine, and you hope there is a good set of managers and partners there to coach you on your career path, which I had. I learned a great deal working in this company and was content for many years. However, at one point, the company changed its executive leadership as a result of many previous bad internal accounting issues. In general the work was fun, and my direct management and leadership were great people, but the firm itself started to lose the value of each employee and focused only on the numbers.

Focusing on the numbers is important, as a company must be managed appropriately, but this company shifted from helping customers to a model run from the CFO's perspective. In fact, the new CEO was the CFO in his previous company. He was brought in to get the finances correct, but as a result of decisions being made 100 percent from the CFO's standpoint, the company ended up devaluing the individual employees and customers at the same time. This significantly affected the company's growth. During the last year, the CEO himself had sent major threats to different partners. They were actually spammed across the entire internal e-mail distribution list for many employees to view.

Threatening an employee is not a good idea for a leader. As leaders we need to cut expenses and inspire new direction at the same time. There must be hope for those willing to stick it out through the hard times. In my experience, it has become clear over multiple situations that at any point when the executive leadership starts to blanket threaten or fire people without providing any hope with new vision, it is a sign of internal company deterioration. It also is a major concern when the company shifts from a customer-driven solution to a solution driven by the CFO, targeting only cost-cutting measures in an effort to please the market. When this happens, the company has lost any connection to its customers as well as to its employees or the value of those individuals. When those star players feel they are no longer valued and there is no hope, they will leave, and then a once-successful company starts a trend downward, and many others will abandon ship too.

An employee's directional energy is another key factor to look for in a company that has misaligned values. This happens often in an organization that is CFO driven. In this case, customers were no longer the primary focus, and all of my energy had been redirected to internal problems. I was forced into a role where I was required to fill out so much internal-audit paperwork based on several broken internal-finance processes that there was little time to focus on my customers and grow the business.

More than once I have seen that when a company redirects the energy of a star A player from growing the company to focusing on inward battles, it may be time to reevaluate the company. Imagine that if instead of trying to score baskets, this great basketball player redirected his energy and started trying to fix other internal problems. He likely would start to lose focus on the game, and the team would not have won so many championships. It is one thing to fix flaws in your coworkers and make them better, but when energy is directed toward fighting internal processes versus seeking improvement, then in most cases, that company has lost the value of the individual contributor. It would have been better to create an entire group to focus on the internal process while working with those external-focusing individuals to set the new company direction, inspire hope, and keep the individual contributor engaged. Finally, after I spent more than six years at this company, when another blanket e-mail from the CEO came out with threats of firing people, I decided my energy was better spent helping someone else versus fighting internal battles against processes and leadership. Within about a two-year period after I left, this CFO-led company, which was a consulting powerhouse at one time, went bankrupt.

Scenario 5: Understanding the Acquisition

From the consulting powerhouse, my career transitioned to a company that had just been purchased by a bigger security company. Because I had seen a few start-ups go bankrupt, there was a sense of nervousness in my bones about going back to another. The next six to seven years of my life were great. This smaller security company was purchased by a larger security company, and the mix turned out to be a success because the larger security corporation listened to those in the smaller company. At this company I connected with some of the best and brightest people in the industry and acquired many lifelong colleagues.

However, at around years five and six, the company was purchased by an even larger non-security-based company. This was a worldwide organization with several hundred thousand workers. A short time after this purchase, I found myself fighting internal battles and political structures again. If this was to continue, I would end up losing my skill and edge in the market because instead of focusing on my passion of security, my energy was redirected toward fighting internal processes. The company's internal legal requirements, global tax practices, and recruiting procedures enforced a corporate structure with overwhelming overhead, which made it impractical to successfully innovate and keep up with the market. All of these items made it very difficult to compete with smaller, more dynamic companies in the same business. Obviously the larger company bought the smaller company for a reason, but sometimes these larger companies forget the reason or try to force change without understanding the differences in the employee culture and the smaller company operating model first.

The larger company really didn't understand the security market and pushed too much change on the smaller organization. Essentially there was so much overhead they paralyzed innovation, which made it hard to compete in some aspects. When I look back, I realize that the larger company's officials really just didn't understand the industry or the acquisition they had made, nor did they listen to those in the smaller company. After several months of trying to push change, it was apparent the company didn't know how to focus on this type of customer or the employees.

Eventually I moved on to another start-up company, where I had more influence and could follow my security passion. A few years after I left, the company that bought my previous company, which had struggled to make ground in the security area, rolled off several parts and eventually the entire security organization. It appears the leaders really didn't understand the market and decided on a different future for both organizations. In any event, this was one of the best company experiences I have lived.

Scenario 6: Can One CEO Represent Too Skilled?

Before we dive into this scenario, it is important to understand the background and the events that led to this point. For the job in this example, I was recruited out of my last company to start up a new services division with several others. There were many choices that I could have taken, but I decided to follow the CEO, who I knew had a previous history of growing companies fast and selling them. In this company the CEO had quickly grown the company substantially in a little more than three years, and the company was starting to feel the pressure. He eventually stepped down as CEO and promoted one of the CEOs from a company that was purchased during his strong growth period. Overall, the three and half years at this job were a roller-coaster ride of success and frustration. However, the company had grown significantly and was no longer in start-up mode. It had been over two years since the IPO, and the company was struggling on several levels. In some aspects, such as the enacting of a blanket optimization effort—in other words, termination—it appeared as if the company was making changes that did not value certain employees.

In a frightening instance of history repeating itself, it looked as if management might be driven from the CFO perspective, announcing publicly a change in direction "to balance growth with profitability" and that there would be "about 300 to 400 positions eliminated." This perspective is very different from the individual- or customer-based perspective that had brought the firm success in the past. It is important for employees to understand that costs need to be addressed, and I believe there are people and proven leadership in the organization that understand the principle of Too Skilled. But will the upper-management-level staff understand how to leverage the key individuals, inspire hope, and build a successful team and organization around those individuals? Will the corporate structure allow for the appropriate individuals to be rewarded before they leave?

Too Skilled requires several prime factors to be in place—otherwise the team or organization will not be a great success (e.g., win the championship). The details of the Too Skilled Factor will be explained in depth in the following chapters, but it is essential that there is an excellent individual with good leadership coaching. Only with that formula is a championship in the future. A famous Scottish writer, Thomas Carlyle, believed in the great-man theory, but the Too Skilled Factor represents two great individuals together.

Unfortunately, sometimes leadership promotes poor employees based on relationships, and the good employees who brought significant value and innovation end up leaving. This is when a leader is on the cusp of ignoring the Too Skilled Factor. With that said, there may be a time when the CEO can embody both aspects of Too Skilled since this individual is the top leader. In this case, the current CEO started his own small firm that was eventually purchased at a significant multiple, and he now has risen to the CEO position of the current company.

Although this question can only be answered in time, it will be interesting to see if the CEO turns out to be the ultimate representation of the Too Skilled Factor in making this company a success. In any event, it still may require the board of directors to fill in as the leadership role.

5. Defining the Factor

Too Skilled is the idea that an individual has a significant positive effect on the outcome of a scenario. The entity with the Too Skilled Factor is the great person of the most importance in a particular situation, balanced with an excellent leader. It's the idea that an individual is an integral part of success, and that individual can affect the outcome of many situations in a positive way, provided the correct structure and leadership are in place. The Too Skilled Factor is the essential element pertaining to success or failure.

To understand the key aspects of the factor, we must display it at the highest level as we would a mathematical equation. In the simplest form, the Too Skilled Factor breaks down into two items: first is a great employee, and second is excellent leadership, as shown in figure 2.

Too Skilled Factor

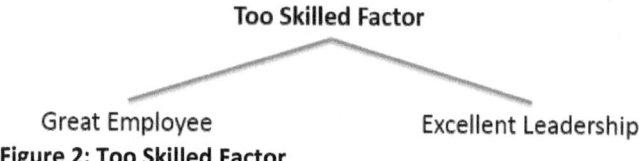

Great Employee   Excellent Leadership

Figure 2: Too Skilled Factor

As mentioned previously, without an employee, there is no one to play the game, but not just any employee will work. The factor is dependent upon those employees who are exceptional at what they do in the workplace. In the New York Times, famous social media CEO Mark Zuckerberg once was quoted saying, "Someone who is exceptional in their role is not just a little better than someone who is pretty good, they are one hundred times better." Ideally, the great employee is someone whom a solution and team can be built around to achieve success. In fact, if the employee is negative and becomes a poison to the team or organization, the opposite effect may also occur.

Taking the first part of the equation, great employee, and continuing to understand its factors is important, as there are several characteristics that make up a great employee. In simple form, a great employee—or, in the case of basketball players, a great athlete—can be factored down further to loyalty and action-oriented, as shown in figure 3.

Figure 3: Too Skilled Factorization

In the analysis of the great basketball player, he was loyal to the team, at least until after retirement. A great employee will exhibit solid traits of loyalty in the beginning, and if the company treats the employee correctly and continues to provide the employee with a believable mission, he or she will remain loyal. Loyal employees are very important, as they bring with them a level of integrity that is the foundation for a good work ethic. Back in 2013, *Forbes* published a list of fifteen traits of the ideal employee. Here is an excerpt from that article: "Honest—An employee can have all the talent in the world, but without integrity and authenticity, nothing great will be accomplished. If nothing else, you want honest, forthright employees at your organization; otherwise your company will turn off clients and ultimately won't survive."

Another component of loyalty is also knowing when the employee is not helping the business. Loyal employees will usually provide information when their involvement is no longer of use, and their energy should be redirected so all parties can move on. Thus, loyalty factors down further to the two important components of integrity and communication.

The second factor of loyalty for the employee is to have solid traits of communication. STACK.com has an article called "5 Traits of Great Basketball Leaders," where communication is listed as one of the main traits. In our great basketball player example, he was of course a leader of his team, and without great communication, he might not have been able to leverage and engage his team members to win so many games. Good communicators improve their business by refocusing their management and coworkers on those items that matter the most to the customer. By leveraging the factor of a customer-focused message, the team will drive toward a common strategy and goal that will leave no one offended. Without customers, there is no court for the game to be played on, and satisfying or not satisfying the customer base will ultimately be the success or end of a company.

A great employee's communication is further factored down into two components: fresh ideas and customer focus, as displayed in figure 3. A company that is knee-deep in problems or in what we call "firefighting mode" sometimes is not able to step away from the problem. A great employee is able to separate him- or herself from the problem and try to see it from an outsider's view. There are many different ways of providing fresh ideas, such as researching a competitor, taking time off, and brainstorming. Typically, focusing on a past experience or the customers' problems will help, which brings us to further factorization of customer focus.

With a customer-focused communication approach and an employee who provides clear messaging from the customer, most problems can be solved in time once the right mix of solutions are pulled together. A customer-focused employee will bring the element of problem visibility to the forefront and promote a good brand image. Like the loyal athlete trying to solve the team's issues, the loyal employee is committed to solving the problem and is passionate about doing right for both the customer and the business. This individual needs the team and leadership coaching support for the company to solve the problem. A loyal employee who is customer focused will review situations and issues objectively, providing the right visibility to help everyone understand the root cause of the problem. A loyal employee will always explain from his or her viewpoint where the problem or problems exist and typically will offer suggestions to those problems. This individual will not be afraid to say if one particular individual is the problem or if there is a complete breakdown in the process or management. This is a critical part of the factorization of a great employee in the overall equation of being successful.

The final element in the factorization of a great employee is brand image. An employee is the company's greatest asset for brand image. Look at the most successful individuals, they are their brand and they become icons. Employees are the first line to the customer and the most trusted asset for customers. Here is an excerpt from the Edelman company about employee trust that emphasizes how customers view your front line: "In fact, in several areas, employees are viewed as the most trusted sources of information, particularly when it comes to communicating on financial earnings and operational performance, a business' practices or handling of a crisis, and how it treats employees and customers. In each of these areas, they outrank a company CEO, senior executive, activist consumer, academic, and media spokesperson as far as trust and credibility."

Customers believe and trust the employees they deal with regularly. Long-term relationships are built over time. When the company stops valuing the great employee, the customer is the first to hear about it, and that impact can be great, resulting in a customer unsure about the company. In some cases, a customer may even shift to a competitive product, which will have an impact on the overall success of the first company. On the other hand, if that employee promotes and believes in the business, then that employee promotes a positive brand image that will drive the company to new sales.

Shifting focus to the other element of a great employee is the factorization of an action-oriented individual. It cannot be summarized much better than in this *Forbes* article on ideal employee traits: "Action-oriented—Hire employees who take action and take chances. While chances may lead to failure, they will more often lead to success and mold confidence while generating new ideas. Stagnant employees won't make your company money; action-oriented employees will."

Action-oriented employees are difficult to find during an interviewing process sometimes. Recruiting individuals who are known to be action oriented is a key factor in the overall equation of success. Typically, those who are action oriented can be further factored down into two components of skill and passion.

Skill, as defined by *Merriam-Webster's Learner's Dictionary*, is the ability to do something that comes from training, experience, or practice. The great basketball player had skill; he worked hard, and after years of practice, he was a refined and experienced player. One cannot assume a person in the early stages of life has a large amount of skill, as skill is obtained over time. After twenty years of experience in an industry, with focus and hard work, one can be very skilled, but there are also many who spend twenty years in a field and still do not have skill because they lack passion and hard work. Skill is an essential component of the Too Skilled Factor; without skill, it cannot be obtained.

Passion, which is the second component of an action-oriented individual, is fundamental to success. Without passion, one does not care about the mission. Without passion, one does not devote the appropriate time or effort to the success of the situation. Michael Jordan was quoted once stating, "Even when I'm old and gray, I won't be able to play it, but I'll still love the game." A passionate individual will move mountains. These individuals don't take no for an answer; they believe there is always a way to solve the problem, and they are keen on figuring it out. Therefore, passion is fundamental to the Too Skilled Factor. Passion also can be further factored down to self-discipline and commitment, as displayed in figure 3.

A self-disciplined individual will do what it takes every day to be great. Michael Jordan said, "Some people want it to happen, some wish it to happen, others make it happen." The self-disciplined employee will make it happen. This individual will spend his or her free time studying and practicing to be the best. This type of person will be consumed by passion day and night. A self-disciplined person will put in the work, and then the results will follow naturally, which will help drive the team and the business to success.

Commitment is the final element in the great employee factorization equation. It is key in the equation. Michael Jordan was quoted in 2005 saying the following: "Uncompromised. You have to be uncompromised in your level of commitment to whatever you are doing, or it can disappear as fast as it appeared…Excellence isn't a one-week or one-year ideal. It's a constant. There will be days when you don't feel on top of your game, or meetings in which you aren't at your best, but your commitment remains constant. No compromises."

Simply said, there are no compromises. As an individual, one must remain committed to complete the mission and be successful. With an action-oriented individual who remains loyal to the work effort, success can be obtained with skill, passion, and hard work.

6. The Leadership Element

Success on the battlefield is changed by the actions of one man. This is the case with the great basketball player in the battlefield of basketball; however, without excellent leadership to guide the success, this player may have never won a championship. As much as all of the folks involved may not like to admit it, there were multiple aspects that were key to the Chicago Bulls' success. It started with one scout who had vision and several other elements. He saw a team built around a great player and recruited others to support this player. The scout was one key element; however, the coach was the leader the team and the individual player needed to complete the equation. The coach not only took the team and this player to six championships, but he also took the Los Angeles Lakers to five championships. The leadership element in the equation is an essential part of the Too Skilled Factor. Without the coach, the Chicago Bulls would no longer win a championship. Leadership in both business and basketball can be broken down into two initial elements of coaching and vision, as shown in figure 3.

Coaching, as displayed by this excellent leader, was an ongoing exercise that was proved to take not only the Bulls, but the Lakers to the championship. In business, coaching employees is no different. There is always great talent, but sometimes with great talent there is inexperience. A great employee can always be better, and coaching is the key to ensuring a skilled employee pushes him- or herself to be the best. Coaching also is the key to helping that individual understand exactly what characteristics make the individual the best. In many cases, it only takes very slight and moderate changes to sharpen an individual's communication, which coaching can help accomplish.

Vision, which was displayed by the basketball scout in his selection of teammates around a star player, is a very important component of leadership that can typically be broken down into timing and innovative solutions. Having an idea and believing in it is key for leadership. The idea convinces the employee that the mission is worth fighting for and that the mission has a greater purpose. Being able to visualize how a team can win the championship, based on putting certain elements together, or being able to see how a business can change the landscape and drive a new market is one key to success as a leader. However, there are many people who have had vision and have not succeeded, because vision alone may not be enough.

Timing is a component of vision that must be in place. For the Chicago Bulls, the timing was perfect. There was a great athlete and an excellent coach. With any other mix, the championship may not have been obtained. For example, the Bulls had many playoff runs with different players, but the factor was not in place until leadership fostered the right changes and empowered a great player.

The second component of vision is to have innovative solutions. In business, a leader must always invent something that is better, faster, and less expensive than the last great item. For example, if we look at Apple again and the invention of its music player, it was such an innovative device for music that it changed the destiny of the company. For years people used these bulky compact disks or cassette players, and here was this small device that had over five gigabytes of music, which was a significant amount over any previous technology. The coach of the Chicago Bulls was also an innovative leader. He was known for using Tex Winter's triangle offense and a Zen-based approach. Innovative solutions can further be factored down in the Too Skilled Factor equation to the two key elements of high retention and satisfied customers.

High retention can be looked at from either the individual employee's or the customers' view. An excellent leader will look at both aspects under innovative solutions. The leader will be able to innovate internal aspects of the company that challenge and excite an employee, which will ensure the customers are happy, which in turn will also help drive brand awareness. Retaining the employee displays a consistent message of stability with continuous progress to the customer, which will keep the customer excited about the future. In addition, the customer will retain a stronger relationship over time with the employee and will provide the necessary feedback that is required to refine the vision. With the data to refine the vision, the company can execute and meet the customer's requirements and satisfy the customer.

A satisfied customer is not always easy to balance, but this customer will bring more demand and increasing revenue to the business, which is the key to success. In reviewing the basketball team example, it is important to understand that even though we have a great player and an excellent coach, it was also the business that succeeded during this time. In fact, *Fortune* magazine stated, "Jordan's overall impact on NBA attendance is $165.5 million."

Not only did this player and his coach change the Bulls—together they changed the entire industry. This happens in business all the time with people like those who started major operating system companies or innovative cars. They all changed the industry in the same way this great player changed basketball, by satisfying the customer, which increased demand and increased the overall revenue of the business.

7. Becoming the Factor

Many individuals are gifted at some aspect of life. In the basketball example, this player was an amazing athlete who, with certain factors in place, changed the game and took his team to multiple championships. He was one major aspect that we can distill to simple elements so we can understand how one person with the right leadership can change an entire business. Unfortunately, none of us are as great as this player at basketball, but each of us can take the key elements within the Too Skilled Factor and do something great with ourselves and possibly our businesses.

Each of us must be committed to a purpose, disciplined to obtain it, and skilled to execute it. Each needs to look at the problems and come up with fresh ideas to solve those problems, thereby promoting a brand image with integrity. With these characteristics, greatness can be obtained.

Leaders must remember to coach the members of their teams and be patient for the right time to execute their solution. A leader must focus on retaining both the best employees and the customers, which will lead to high demand and revenue if the leader is listening and executing with the team in place.

Company leaders need to listen to their employees and support their values. They need to recognize those individuals who have the Too Skilled Factor. Only then can a leader take action to make the necessary changes for those employees and the company to succeed and make their marks on history.

References

"10 Amazing Success Lessons from Michael Jordan." *Pick the Brain* (blog), October 14, 2010. Accessed August 11, 2016. http://www.pickthebrain.com/blog/10-amazing-success-lessons-from-michael-jordan/.

"15 Traits of the Ideal Employee." *Forbes*, April 2, 2013. Accessed August 23, 2016. http://www.forbes.com/sites/kensundheim/2013/04/02/15-traits-of-the-ideal-employee/#7c0bfd217c94.

"2016 Edelman TRUST BAROMETER » Executive Summary." Edelman. January 17, 2016. Accessed August 23, 2016. http://www.edelman.com/insights/intellectual-property/2016-edelman-trust-barometer/executive-summary/.

"The Birth of the iPod." *Macworld*, October 23, 2011. Accessed August 22, 2016. http://www.macworld.com/article/1163181/ipods/the-birth-of-the-iPod.html.

Campbell, Courtney. "5 Traits of Great Basketball Leaders." STACK. June 1, 2012. Accessed March 30, 2017. http://www.stack.com/a/traits-of-basketball-leaders.

"Chicago Bulls." Wikipedia. March 25, 2017.
Accessed August 5, 2016.
https://en.wikipedia.org/wiki/Chicago_Bulls
#1984.E80.80.:_The_Michael_Jordan_era.

"For Buyers of Web Start-Ups, Quest to Corral
Young Talent." *New York Times*, May 17,
2011. Accessed February 23, 2017.
http://www.nytimes.com/2011/05/18/technol
ogy/18talent.html.

"Great Man Theory." Wikipedia. March 2, 2017.
Accessed February 23, 2017.
https://en.wikipedia.org/wiki/Great_Man_th
eory.

"Jerry Krause." Wikipedia. Accessed August 9,
2016.
https://en.wikipedia.org/wiki/Jerry_Kraus.

"The Jordan Effect: The World's Greatest
Basketball Player Is Also One of Its Great
Brands. What Is His Impact on the
Economy?" *Fortune*, June 22, 1998.
Accessed August 9, 2016.
http://archive.fortune.com/magazines/fortun
e/fortune_archive/1998/06/22/244166/index.
htm.

Owens, Jeremy C. "FireEye Plans Layoffs as New
CEO Takes the Helm, Stock Plunges."
MarketWatch. August 5, 2016. Accessed
December 23, 2016.

http://www.marketwatch.com/story/fireeye-plans-layoffs-as-new-ceo-takes-the-helm-2016-08-04.

"Phil Jackson." Wikipedia. Accessed August 8, 2016. https://en.wikipedia.org/wiki/Phil_Jackson.

PRNewswire. October 24, 2005. Accessed August 9, 2016. http://www.prnewswire.com/news-releases/driven-from-within—michael-jordan-55543952.html.

"Small Business Employee Benefits and HR Blog: Employee Retention—the Real Cost of Losing an Employee." *ZaneBenefits* (blog), February 4, 2016. Accessed December 14, 2016. https://www.zanebenefits.com/blog/bid/312123/employee-retention-the-real-cost-of-losing-an-employee.

About the Author

Jason Bevis is a security professional with more than twenty years of experience working in many start-ups and large corporations. He has been through multiple IPOs and worked at several companies purchased by larger companies. He has worked for top security firms including Foundstone, a division of McAfee, a subsidiary of Intel; Mandiant, a division of FireEye; KPMG consulting; and Hewlett Packard, among others. During his career, he has held many positions of leadership, including managing small elite teams to larger leadership roles ranging from thirty to fifty reports. In many cases, Jason was fully accountable for running the entire function or functions within the organization. He has an excellent track record with low attrition rates and has built extensive programs for onboarding new hires.

In recent years, he moved into engineering and product management after successfully building a security integration automation platform with his team. He attributes much of his success to leveraging the right employees in the right situations. Over his career, he has continually referred to the "Too Skilled Factor" in its original form as a common phrase to inspire his employees and coworkers to help obtain a successful outcome.